Anglican

I Belong

Parent's Guide

*'I have come that they may have life,
an abundance of life.'*

Anglican I Belong
First Holy Communion Programme

Published by Redemptorist Publications

Text: Aileen Urquhart
Adapted and edited by Revd. Jill Talbot-Ponsonby
Illustration and Design: Lis Davis

First Published   April 2001
Reprinted   September 2002

ISBN 0 85231 242 3

Printed by Collier Litho Ltd., Romford, RM6 5SD

Redemptorist PUBLICATIONS

Alphonsus House Chawton Hampshire GU34 3HQ
Telephone 01420 88222   Fax 01420 88805
rp@ShineOnline.net   www.ShineOnline.net

Dear Parent,

Welcome to I Belong! Whether this is your first experience of preparation for *First Holy Communion* or not, you may be interested to know about the thinking behind I Belong.

It seems to me that spirituality, to be valid, has to be grounded in the reality in which we live. This reality is what we see, hear and touch in our daily lives, as well as the overarching reality of "what the eye has not seen, nor ear heard, nor the human heart conceived" 1 Corinthians 2:9

Genuine spirituality will accept both realities at white-hot heat, and find that somehow they are fused (confused seems the wrong word), and we find that the very dirt we walk on is Holy Ground indeed.

Everyday Experience

This programme is therefore very much based on everyday experience, and encourages you and your child to find the deeper realities behind everyday experiences such as eating, working, making up after a row etc. During each session with you, and then with the children, the leader explores one of the themes.

The themes are ones that unfold naturally during the celebration of the Eucharist - parenthood, mercy, glory, etc - and extra light is shed on the theme by looking at the Bible. But the themes start and finish with everyday experience. Hopefully the second look will be enriched by everything we share about the Eucharist, Church and Bible during the session.

Communication

At this important time for your child and your family it is important to meet together regularly if this is possible. Not only will you receive the practical details that need communicating, but more importantly you have a wonderful opportunity to get to grips with the theme by hearing other people's insights and difficulties. The questions and reflections you and your child experience will almost certainly be what is on the minds of other parents and children. If you do not know many people in your parish, you now have a wonderful chance to get to know the First Communion families really well. The community aspect of the Eucharist is much more obvious when you are in a distinct community already.

The beauty of basing the sessions on personal experience is that there are no right or wrong answers. If someone says he has never experienced the glory of God's presence this is a valid comment. If someone says she gasps in wonder every time she sees a rainbow this is valid also. In this instance the task of the leader is to reach, and enable the group to reach, a greater understanding of the glory of God. Listening to one another, to what the Bible says, what the Church says, listening to the Spirit stirring within us, will bring about the understanding. An understanding of the heart more than one of the intellect.

Your own spiritual life

Of course, knowledge is necessary, and it is important to know what the Bible and the Church are saying to us. Reading the Bible prayerfully is very important. You probably have your own selection of good spiritual writers that inspire you.

Above all, it is important to PRAY. If you are busy, and most people are these days, it is easy to put off any serious attempt at prayer, and just get by with a few quick words and a promise to 'do better tomorrow'. I find that tomorrow is just as busy as today, and my life is a series of promises to God. However I still believe that prayer is the most important thing we can do to improve the quality of teaching. I am going to stop making promises to God, and actually spend some 'quality' time praying now!

I hope you enjoy using 'I Belong'. I hope it helps you, and your child, to grow in the love of Jesus, present in the bread and wine, present in one another. After all, this is what is at the heart of our faith, isn't it?

God bless your work.

Aileen B. Urquhart

Aileen B. Urquhart

Contents

Introduction

I Belong is a preparation journey which is based on the framework of our celebration of the Eucharist. All the material is firmly grounded in the Bible. Full references are given for your preparation of each section.

'I have come that they may have life, an abundance of life.'

Each session the children will be exploring a
theme connected with the Eucharist.
They will start by looking at their ordinary
experiences of the theme — beginning with
Names and **Parents** — and then go on to think
about the theme in Scripture, and in Church.
Finally, they will look again at everyday
experiences, and hopefully discover how the
Eucharist is about **REAL LIFE**.

SESSION 1 IN THE NAME OF THE FATHER

Your child's preparation for First Holy Communion begins with this first session which focuses on **names**. We will also be talking about **baptism**.

Page 3 Everyday Life

The names we are called can affect us deeply. You probably spent a long time choosing a name for your child. It had to be just right. You may also remember suffering as a child if you were constantly called names such as lazy-bones, or heard your parents label you in some way or another.

Pages 4 to 6 Scripture

In scripture, the use of names is often very significant. Adam (the name means of the earth) represents all of us, men and women alike. The link with earth is not to be despised. Creation is glorious. Genesis tells us that God saw creation was good … good … very good. Adam's naming of animals means that we have power, and therefore responsibility, over the rest of creation.

At the Annunciation God became part of this glorious creation, thus making it even more magnificent. By becoming human, God became subject to other human beings, and was also *named*. The name Jesus (Joshua) means *saviour*. In the *Old Testament*, Joshua was one who led the Israelites over the River Jordan into the freedom of the Promised Land after their forty years in the desert. It was not by accident that Jesus was baptised in the Jordan. He is the true Joshua, leading us all to fulfilment and life.

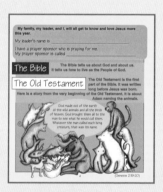

The baptism of Jesus also has links with the story of creation. Just as in *Genesis* the Spirit of God hovered over the waters of chaos and brought forth life, so the Spirit hovered over Jesus. Jesus is the *second Adam* - the new creation. In Adam, we walk in friendship with God. In Jesus, we are re-created as children of God.

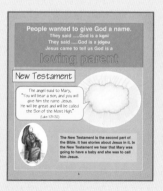

Page 8 Picture to colour in

Page 9 Church

For Jesus, his baptism was a powerful sign of his sonship. He experienced God as *Father*, and this experience was to colour everything he said and did. In baptism, we are saying many things. We are not only celebrating the new life - the new *Adam* - that has been brought into the world, but also joining Jesus in his *Abba-experience*. Baptism is the Spirit breathing life into the chaos, it is the crossing over the waters of Jordan into a new life of liberty, it is God calling us his beloved children.

It is our baptism that gives us the right to come together as Church. It unites us all as children of God - all equal - all loved.

Page 10 Everyday Life

It would be wonderful to be constantly aware of our dignity as children of God. So often we put ourselves down. *'Oh I'm so stupid,' 'Oh you are a nuisance.'* Perhaps we could start saying nice things about ourselves and others. We are all God's beloved children.

At home you might like to go through the *Our Father* with your child, explaining some of the more difficult words. If you don't say night prayers together this could be a good time to start. You could also talk about his/her baptism. If you had a party at the time, tell your child about it. Much of the scripture that we will be looking at during the next few months will mention parties and celebrations, and it will all be leading up to the celebration of your child's **First Holy Communion**.

Encourage your child to use their book.

LORD HAVE MERCY

This session the children will be thinking about **mercy** in everyday life, scripture, and church. Hopefully they will come to a better understanding of the mercy of God, and how we are called to be merciful in our day to day dealings with people. At the Eucharist we come before our loving God to receive infinite mercy, and are challenged and empowered to pass on this gift so freely and lovingly given.

Page 14 Everyday life

Children are completely dependent on the merciful love of adults. Their concept of mercy will depend on the experience of mercy that they receive from US. God is traditionally portrayed as a father. Their idea of God will be based on the parenting they receive from US. If we forgive them willingly, and forget past bad behaviour, they will grow up with confidence in life, and in the God who gave us life.

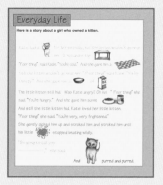

Page 16 Old Testament

The creation stories in the Bible were written in about 1,000 B.C. King David had united the tribes into one kingdom and there was relative peace and prosperity. People had time to think about the meaning of life, and other big questions such as the problem of suffering and evil. Under the inspiration of God *Genesis* was written. What it contains is not *scientific* truth but *theological* truth. The story of the serpent and the forbidden fruit acknowledges that although wonderfully created, we all struggle with the temptation towards evil. However, this basic weakness of ours shows God's wonderful mercy towards us, in the promise of a Saviour. Every year during the Easter Vigil we hear the sin of Adam called a *'happy fault'*.

Page 17 New Testament

We will be looking closely at the story of the Prodigal Son at the parents' sessions. There is a bit of each character in the story in all of us. We can in turn be the forgiving father, the tearaway younger son and the self-righteous elder brother. A good book on this is *'The Return of the Prodigal Son'* by Henri Nouwen.

Page 19 Picture to colour in

Page 20 Church

We say *Lord Have Mercy - Kyrie Eleison* at the Eucharist. Some scholars say the word *eleison* comes from the word for olive. The *mercy* we receive from God is like the olive twig symbol of hope, that the dove brought to Noah when the flood waters subsided. We can imagine the Prodigal Son being freshly bathed and anointed with oil of the olives before he put on the new robes, sandals and ring. We are reminded of the anointing of priests and kings in the Bible, and of our own anointing as holy and royal people at our baptism. This rich abundance is what we expect from God when we ask for *mercy*.

Read *'School for Prayer'* by *Archbishop Anthony Bloom* for more about this.

Page 21 Everyday life

There is a playground game called *'Mercy, Mercy'* in which one child squeezes another child's finger until s/he cries for mercy. This is not what we mean by mercy. We mean something altogether more positive, more like an aromatherapy massage. Shakespeare puts it like this:

'The quality of mercy is not strained; It droppeth as the gentle rain from heaven upon the place beneath. It is twice blest: it blesseth him that gives and him that takes.

'Tis mightiest in the mightiest; it becomes the throned monarch better than his crown;…

It is enthroned in the hearts of kings, It is an attribute of God himself…'

Merchant of Venice, Act IV Sc 1

SESSION 3
CONFESSION

CELEBRATING OUR RESCUE

This is the first of two sessions about Confession in order to help the children take part in the general confession at Holy Communion. In this session the children are helped to understand the need to confess their sins and how God rescues them from sin.

In the second session they will begin to think about how God helps them 'get it right' and continue to get it right.

The need to own up when we've done wrong is part of everyday life and is one of the hardest parts of living. When we deal with our mistakes honestly and begin to put them right we begin a wonderful new relationship with God. Being able to confess and know we are forgiven is an opportunity for praise and thanksgiving to God for his help and understanding.

Page 25 Everyday life

You could remind your child of any rescue they have seen. Maybe a road accident or fire. Perhaps they tried to rescue a bird fallen out of a tree, or stood up for a younger child when they were being bullied. If your child has ever been lost, you could discuss how they felt. (The odds are **YOU** were even more worried than they were!) Use this as an illustration of how pleased God is when we are back on the right path.

What we need to get across to the children is that **they are basically GOOD, and that sometimes they lose their way and need 'rescuing',** not that they are sinful and need constant correcting, in order that they will occasionally be good and loveable.

Page 27 Old Testament

In the past, our picture of God has sometimes been distorted. Because people have seen God as all-holy, perfect, etc. they have stressed the distance between God and human beings, and dwelt on our sinfulness and unworthiness. We need to get back to the image of God as a loving parent, and see ourselves as made in the image and likeness of God. As we said last session, God is Emmanuel - God with us. *'Can a mother forget her child? Even if she did, I would not forget you.'* (Isaiah 49:15)

Page 28 New Testament

The Parable of the Lost Sheep is one of three parables - (the Lost Sheep, the Lost Coin, the Prodigal Son) all together in Luke's Gospel - about God's joy over returning sinners. They are three stories told to the self-righteous scribes and Pharisees who were disgusted at Jesus because he mixed with 'publicans and sinners'. In Jewish law, certain occupations automatically made people sinners, as you were unable to keep the outward observances of the law.

Page 29 Picture to colour

Pages 30 Everyday Life again

The children will be thinking about feelings, and how they are useful signals to their needs. At home you are good shepherds to your children when you empathise with their anger, hurt, envy, etc. and rescue them by helping them find good ways of dealing with their problems. Never say to your child *'I WON'T LOVE/LIKE YOU IF...'* Apart from being a devastating statement, it is not a true reflection of God's parenthood. GOD IS LOVE.

Page 31 Church

For many Christians there has been a tendency to stress the distance between God and us, so that the need for confession and forgiveness is a very negative experience.

Try to underline the 'celebration' aspect of confession with your child.

We can rejoice in the fact that God's love is unconditional. God's love knows no limits it is there for us at all times. In the Eucharist we are celebrating God's forgiving love and on-going help.

SESSION 4 GOD HELPS ME GET IT RIGHT
CONFESSION

At our last session we thought about how God rescues us from past failings, and how confession and forgiveness is going on in life all the time. We can celebrate the fact that when we confess to God, then because of God's love for us we are forgiven.

In this session we continue to celebrate God's forgiving love but this time with a focus on the future. Knowing we are loved by God all the time, even when we get things wrong, should enable us to grow and change. With God's help our failure can be overcome.

Page 37 Everyday life

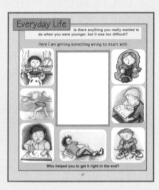

Remind the children about achievements like learning to swim, ride a bike, read a book. A lot of mistakes went into each process, but you were there to encourage and help. It is probably your experience that any time you were impatient or uninterested in their struggles they did not do very well, and even shrivelled up a bit, but when you gave your whole-hearted attention to their struggle they seemed to blossom. God is the good parent, who encourages us even when we fail. God's belief in us gives us the courage to believe in ourselves. God says, *'Go on, I know you can do it,'* and we find it is true.

Page 40 New Testament

The children have had two parables about forgiveness already — The Prodigal Son and the Lost Sheep. Each story ends with a party - a celebration that what was lost is now found. They are now hearing about a real-life situation when Jesus **'practises what he preaches'**. Jesus searches out the lost son of Abraham and the celebration itself brings about the wonderful transformation in Zacchaeus.

Zacchaeus, the tax collector, was a collaborator with the Roman authorities, so was considered a traitor by the 'decent' people. Tax collectors collected the money that the Romans exacted, but they were allowed to collect any amount they liked and they pocketed the difference. It was this man whom Jesus singled out to dine with. The effect on Zacchaeus was remarkable. Having been affirmed by Jesus, he confessed his guilt and decided to make amends. His offer to pay back four times what he had wrongly taken was a direct reference to the Jewish law - he was acting as a good Jew now not as a public sinner, for as Jesus said of him, *'This man too is a son of Abraham.'* The message for us is — if we treat our children as sons and daughters of God they will act like sons and daughters of God.

Page 41 Picture to colour in

Pages 42 to 44 The Sacrament

These pages have a lot of reading for the children, and in their sessions they will not have time to discuss all the points. Please go through them with your child, so they are quite confident as to what the prayer of confession is all about. You will notice that the emphasis is very positive. We are thanking God for his forgiveness, and asking help for the future. God really does believe in us (we are made in God's image after all!) and says to us, as Jesus said to the woman taken in adultery, *'Go, and sin no more.'*

Finally — enjoy your child's First Communion. It is a celebration, just as Baptism, Confirmation, Marriage and Ordination, are celebrations.

SESSION 5 GLORY TO GOD IN THE HIGHEST

This session the children will be thinking about **glory**. This is a difficult concept, but a very important one. Everything Jesus did was for the **GLORY** of his Father, and to follow in his footsteps all our actions should also be for the **honour** and **glory** of God.

Page 49 Everyday Life

The children may not have had many experiences of, actually receiving GLORY, but they may well have had experiences which leave them gasping with wonder. A magnificent fireworks display, or the first time they see snow are two possibilities among thousands.

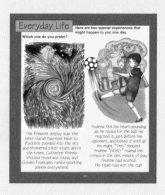

Page 51 Old Testament

The **GLORY** *(shekinah)* of God is spoken of again and again in the Old Testament. In the burning bush episode we learn that we cannot name God *(I Am who I Am)* for God is beyond us.

However we learn that this **HOLY GOD** is a God who **SAVES**. God led the slaves through the desert to freedom, the *shekinah* remaining with them as a pillar of fire by night, and of cloud by day.

Page 52 New Testament

Just as Moses the shepherd saw the **GLORY** of the Lord on the mountain, so did the shepherds of Bethlehem see the **GLORY** on the hills of Bethlehem. Just like Moses, they were afraid, and yet once again there is a message of deliverance from God. Shepherds were *outside the law* as far as respectable people were concerned. They were unable to keep the strict laws of washing which the Pharisees had imposed on the people, and so were imprisoned in a *'sinful'* condition. Once again God approaches people caught up in slavery, and gives them the Good News of peace. God is with us — Emmanuel.

Page 54 Picture to Colour in

Page 55 Church

The whole of the Eucharist is a prayer of praise and thanks to the **GLORY** of God. (*The word* Eucharist *means* **thank you**. *In Greece today you can still hear people saying* **efcharisto - thank you**.)

At the Eucharist the children could listen out for how many times the word **GLORY**, and similar words are mentioned. In their session they will be thinking about the **GLORIA**, but there are other important prayers of praise. The words of the Preface change, according to what aspect of God's glory we are praising and being thankful for. There is also the beautiful prayer,

> **Through him, with him, and in him,**
> **in the unity the Holy Spirit,**
> **all honour and glory are yours, almighty Father**
> **for ever and ever. Amen.**

The response of AMEN is everyone's chance to make the prayer their own. The sound should bring the roof down! The children could be encouraged to really shout it out!

When the shepherds left the magnificent glory of God on the hillside, they arrived at the quiet glory of a baby in a manger. At the Eucharist we meet the quiet glory of God in the bread and wine. The more we are aware of the wonder of the **REAL PRESENCE** the more will our children appreciate this breath-taking **MYSTERY OF FAITH.**

56 Everyday life

St Irenaeus said *'The glory of God is a human being fully alive.'* This is seen most powerfully in Jesus, but the glory of God is also shining in each one of us. We and our children are burning bushes. When we approach one another we approach Holy Ground. Let us teach our children to reverence the holiness of others. To love God and to love our neighbour are two sides of the same coin.

SESSION 6 THIS IS THE WORD OF THE LORD

In this session the children will be thinking about listening to the Word of God. The first half of the Eucharist is called the Liturgy of the Word, and what we listen to focuses our minds on a particular reason for glorifying God, depending on the season of the Church's year, the feast, etc.

Page 61 Everyday life

The children have a 'fun' start this session, thinking about how animals would survive without ears! They will then think about how well they themselves would survive if they didn't **LISTEN**. (The leaders are aware that some children may have hearing problems, and will be sensitive to this.) The idea is to help them consider how listening to the Word of the Lord helps us to live in confidence as children of God.

Page 63 Old Testament

The children read the story of Samuel in the Temple. Hannah had wept and prayed for a child, and promised him to the Lord if she should have one. When Samuel was born, Hannah sang a song of praise to God, recounting the marvellous saving works of God in lifting up the poor and feeding the hungry. Years later, Mary would use this song as a basis for her song of praise to God, when her cousin Elizabeth acknowledged the presence of the Saviour in Mary's womb. This prayer, known as the **Magnificat**, is still used every evening at Evensong.

The children will concentrate on the story of Samuel hearing God call him in the night. The children are like Samuel (and Jesus) in that they are gifts from God. Baptism not only marks their entry into the community, but also makes them **'prophets'** who hear God's word and carry it out to others, just as Samuel (and, of course, Jesus) did. Holy Communion will mark their entry into full membership of the community and as well as making them holy, will give them strength to be prophets: pro-God and pro-others.

Page 65 New Testament

In the Old Testament, there were many prophets who brought God's word to the people. Jesus is more than the greatest of the prophets - he **IS** God's Word. Jesus is the *embodiment* of God. God responds to our poverty and need by becoming poor and needy. God is indeed *Emmanuel — 'God with us'*.

The word *'Bethlehem'* means 'House of Bread'. In Jesus the songs of Hannah and Mary are fulfilled, for in him God comes to our rescue - the poor and hungry are fed.

The promise is kept today in the Eucharist when God is with us as the Bread of Life, and we go out from the Eucharist with a mission to feed the hungry - to be Saviours ourselves to those in need.

Page 66 Picture to colour in

Page 67 Church

The readings at the Eucharist are often above the heads of the children and they can be bored.

One way to help with this would be to get a children's Bible where the readings are simplified and could be read together after the service, allowing time as a family to talk over the readings. Another suggestion to focus their minds on the Eucharist is to take one word — e.g. *glory* or *Father* and listen out for it during the service. This can be helpful for adults as well.

Page 68 Everyday Life

The children are finishing with a Snakes and Ladders type game, where they go up a Ladder if they listen to good/nice things, and down a Snake if they don't listen (or listen to bad ideas!) Please play it at home with your children. It is giving them the message that what we listen to affects us.

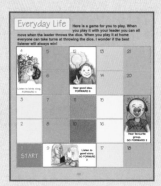

BREAD TO OFFER

Until now the children were thinking about the first part of the Eucharist — the Liturgy of the Word. They are now turning to the second part — the **Liturgy of the Eucharist**. In this session the children will be thinking about the Preparation of the Gifts/Offertory.

Page 73 Everyday Life

You will have more time than the leaders to discuss with your child all that has to happen before a meal can take place. You could think about some of the products you eat, the danger the fishermen undergo, the length of time the farmer has to care for his crop, etc. Perhaps you could work out how many hours' work the food on your table costs!

Page 75 Old Testament

The people in the desert were entirely at the mercy of God (and the heat, lack of food and water etc.) In their wanderings they learnt to trust that God would provide, and developed a real understanding of what *'bread'* stands for. To a large extent we have lost this understanding, and maybe, even, lost a realisation of how dependent we are on God. When hardships hit us we can either grumble, like the Israelites did at first, or develop an attitude of trust in God, who **'gives us our daily bread'**.

The lsraelites were instructed to gather only enough for their daily needs. If they gathered too much the manna putrefied. However the day before the Sabbath they were instructed to gather twice as much so they could rest on the Sabbath. This amount did not putrefy and they were able to eat on the day of rest. Throughout their journey the Israelites were fed on the manna, rather like we, the new People of God, are fed on the bread of life throughout our life's journey. (*Exodus 16*)

Page 77 New Testament

Three of the gospels, Matthew, Mark and Luke, give accounts of the Last Supper of Jesus. John does not. Instead, he puts his teaching about the Eucharist in Chapter 6, the Feeding of the Five Thousand. The children will be thinking about the little boy who offered up his five loaves and two fishes. Jesus took these, and enabled his disciples to feed the crowd, with twelve baskets of scraps left over. As adults, we can go deeper into the mystery, and read all that Jesus said about himself after this great **'sign'**. One thing worth mentioning is that Jesus said, *"I am the Bread of Life."* He makes seven **"I AM"** statements in John's gospel. You may remember that when Moses asked God's name he was told **"I AM WHO I AM."** Jesus is telling us that he, God the great I AM, is feeding us with his own self, and we shall live forever.

Page 78 Picture to colour in

Page 79 Church

As said earlier, we are probably out of touch with the deep significance of presenting bread to God. We are so dependent on food that we are offering God our very existence. To put it less grandly, when we offer up the bread it stands for all the sweat and labour, the tedium of the past week - everything we do to keep a roof above our heads and the wolf from the door. The offering of the money is also deeply significant. It is not an interruption of the Eucharist, but very much part of it. At the beginning of the Bible, in Genesis 14, Melchizedech, the king of Salem and Priest of God Most High, offered bread and wine to God, and Abram (later called Abraham) gave him a tenth of all his wealth.

We will think about the wine next time.

Page 80 Everyday Life

Just as the disciples fed the crowds with the bread, we go out to others to **feed the world**. Our gratitude to God opens up a spirit of generosity in us, and the Eucharist not only feeds us but empowers us to go out to others.

SESSION 8   FRUIT OF THE VINE

In this session the children will be thinking about the wine we use at the Eucharist, and why we use it. As adults we can understand that wine not only symbolises celebration, but that it also stands for sorrow — we talk of a cup of sorrow. If we share a cup with someone we are intimately connected with them. We share their destiny. Although the children will touch on the sorrowful aspect, they will be concentrating on the joy of celebrations.

Page 85 Everyday Life

Often children don't like the taste of wine, so on their first page they will be thinking about tastes they didn't like when they were younger, but do like now. This links in with the idea of **'sacrifice'** in the wine. They had to give up the comfort of a bottle in order to appreciate other drinks/food. Hopefully it will also prepare them for the practicalities of drinking wine at their First Eucharist and afterwards. At home you might like them to taste wine if they haven't yet done so. Communion wine is usually sweet and rich.

Page 87 Old Testament

a) The Passover feast was held every spring to celebrate the deliverance from slavery of the People of God. The feast was not just held in memory of the past. To the Jews, celebrating this feast makes God's saving action present and available to them in the here and now.

b) The People of God thought of themselves as the vineyard of God. Other references to themselves as God's vineyard are Psalm 80 - *'You have brought a grapevine out of Egypt … Turn to us Almighty God … Come and save this grapevine that you planted.'*

Page 89 New Testament

The children will think about the celebration that Jesus provided. So many gallons of wine is really lavish - rather like the miracle of the loaves and fishes when twelve baskets were left over! The abundance of wine is a symbol that the fullness of the Kingdom has arrived (Isaiah 25:6). As adults, we can read more into the miracle (sign). It was *'on the third day'* (links with the Resurrection). Jesus took the water (standing for the old ritualism of the original Covenant) and changed it into wine, standing for the wine of the New Covenant.

Page 91 Picture to colour in

Page 92 Church

a) The link between the Jewish Passover and the Eucharist is very obvious in the Passover prayer (on page 87 in the children's book). The Eucharist is very much a Thank You prayer for all the good things of creation.

b) We also think of ourselves as a vine. Jesus said he was the vine and we are the branches. He is not separate from us - a vine IS the branches - we are the New Risen Body of Christ. *"Whatever you do to the least one of these, you do it to me,"* said Jesus.

c) Just as the Passover makes God's action present for the Jews, so the Eucharist makes God's action present for us. We are liberated from the slavery to sin by receiving the life of Christ. We not only look to the past, to Christ's redeeming acts of death and resurrection, but also to the future. At the Last Supper Jesus said he would not drink again till he drank the new wine of the Kingdom of God. At the Eucharist we bring about the Wedding Feast of the Lamb, and God eats with the New People of God.

Page 93 and 94 Everyday Life

The Kingdom of God will not come about unless we take the Eucharist seriously. Properly understood, the Eucharist means that we join with Jesus in bringing the Good News to the world no matter what the cost.

In the Eucharist we are uniting ourselves to the selfless love of Jesus in giving up his life for his friends. *"No one has greater love than he who gives up his life for his friends."*

(John 15:13) This is exactly what Jesus did.

SESSION 9 **DO THIS IN REMEMBRANCE OF ME**

We now come to the heart of the Eucharist — the 'Institution Narrative'. At this point of the Eucharist the Holy Spirit is invoked: "grant that by the power of your Holy Spirit these gifts of bread and wine may be to us his body and blood" **and then the Words of Consecration are said. Jesus is made present on the altar in a new way. His presence remains in the consecrated hosts reserved in the aumbry (the small cupboard in the wall next to the altar, with a light hanging next to it). He is already present as God, in Scripture, in the priest and the people but this new presence in the sacrament is very special and is called the Real Presence. In the sacrament Christ is present in a unique way, whole and entire, God and man, substantially and permanently.**

Page 99 Everyday Life

We have meals for all sorts of reasons - for comfort, because we are hungry, to sustain us, to celebrate, to sit down and relax etc. Meals can be quick snacks in railway cafes, where we pay more attention to our luggage than the food and company, a great banquet in honour of someone special, an impromptu barbecue when friends call, a relaxing gathering of the family.

Some meals really change us in some way. Sharing the same food and conversation can bring us closer together, and we gain new insights into each other and into the topics of conversation.

Page 101 Old Testament

There is only half a page on the Old Testament in this session, as we are concentrating more on the Last Supper, and we have talked about the Passover before. However it might be worth noting that the word Passover comes from the fact that the Israelites sacrificed a lamb, and put the blood on their door-posts so that God **'passed over'** their houses. Because of the blood of the lamb the Israelites did not suffer the tenth plague - the death of the eldest son. (We are not covering this with the children).

Page 102 New Testament

Jesus took an existing feast, the most important of the Jewish celebrations, and changed it into something new. Throughout the Old Testament, God is constantly renewing the Covenant made with human beings. In the Book of Jeremiah, God promises a New Covenant, not like the previous one. In the New Covenant:

"I will put my law within them. I will write it upon their hearts and I will be their God and they shall be my people … they shall all know me, from the least of them to the greatest. I will forgive them and forget their sins." (*Jeremiah 31:31-34*)

Jesus brought about this New Covenant at his Last Supper when he, the new Lamb of God, offered his life, present in the bread and in the Cup of Salvation (*the Blood of the New Covenant*).

Once again, we are not mentioning 'blood' to the children, although we are talking about Jesus dying for us. In Western Europe, we usually associate *blood* with *death*; for the Jews, *blood* meant *life*.

Page 104 Picture to colour in

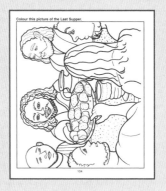

Page 105 Church

At the Eucharist, help your child listen out for the words of Consecration, and the Lamb of God. Don't try to go into long explanations of how Christ is present if they ask **HOW**. Just remember that the presence isn't that of a physical body. (In the next session we will look at how, after the Resurrection, Jesus' body was so transformed he could pass through locked doors and his friends didn't recognise him!) The mystery of Christ present in the Eucharist is so amazing it is called **THE MYSTERY OF FAITH.**

Page 106 Everyday Life

Enjoy your meals together. Make them life-giving occasions!

SESSION 10 BODY OF CHRIST

This session we are looking at the words the priest says as he distributes the host and the cup — 'The Body of Christ' and 'The Blood of Christ'. We are thinking about HOW Christ is present in the bread and wine.

Page 111 Everyday Life

The children will be thinking about how tadpoles and caterpillars change into frogs and butterflies. The outer appearances change, but the inner reality is the same. They will be led to how the opposite happens at the Eucharist. How the outer appearances of the bread and wine are the same, but the inner reality is different.

Old Testament

There is no Old Testament story this session in order to have two New Testament stories. The Old Testament stories have been leading up to this fulfilment of God's promise in the New Covenant.

Pages 114 to 116 New Testament

The two stories (Christ appearing to Mary Magdalen, and to the friends on the way to Emmaus) have been chosen to illustrate the fact that he looked different. He had a different kind of body. At home you could remind your children of Christ's appearances in the Upper Room, first when Thomas was absent, then when he was there. Christ's body could go through locked doors, but he wasn't a ghost - he ate with them, and Thomas could touch him. After the Resurrection Jesus could appear as a gardener, a stranger, he could come and go suddenly and mysteriously. He was not limited by the normal constraints of human life. And yet, it was the same Jesus whom they knew and loved. At Emmaus, the friends recognised him in the *'breaking of the bread'* - in the Eucharist.

Page 115 Picture to colour in

Page 117 Church

It is in the Eucharist that we recognise him too. We look at the outward appearances of bread and wine, but recognise Jesus in the **'breaking of the bread'**. Don't try to go into long explanations of how Christ is present. It is such a unique mystery it is called **THE MYSTERY OF FAITH**. Technical explanations might take away the wonder of it all, rather like explaining how rainbows occur at the very moment the child has been surprised by one. The introduction about tadpoles and caterpillars is more about the wonder of the changes that they can see, to prepare them for the wonder of the change that they can't see.

Page 118 Everyday life

There is so much to say, and so little time! When we go to the Eucharist sometimes we feel wonderful, sometimes we feel hypocritical, sometimes we feel we have the strength to conquer the world afterwards, sometimes we go back to old bad habits. The truth of it is that we are a wounded people just as Jesus was wounded. If we could try to look at one another in the community, and indeed in the world, and see this new Body of Christ, and love one another with the compassion of Christ, the Eucharist will have borne fruit. There will be more about this aspect of the Eucharist in the next session, but for this one, in the last week or so before your child's communion, encourage them to pray quietly to Jesus, and pray together as a family if you feel you can do so. Bearing in mind that they may not feel anything very much after their First Holy Communion (there's a lot of practicalities for them to think about, and they might be nervous), tell them that the time after receiving the Eucharist is a very special time, both for them and Jesus. Time spent in stillness and reverence will help them *'recognise him in the breaking of the bread.'*

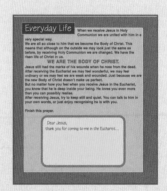

TO LOVE AND SERVE

Our last session of the programme! This will be a shorter session than the earlier ones to allow time for a party at the end. Please encourage your child to finish their book at home. We will be concentrating on getting the children to write a **'thank you letter'** to their Prayer Sponsors. Some of you may have already asked your children to do this. Your child will also be given the name of a new child for them to pray for next year.

Page 123 Everyday Life

At meal times you could make the link between everyday food and spiritual food. Communion gives us strength for living as Christians. If we don't eat of this food regularly we are (literally) not in communion with the Body of Christ. The Eucharist is called the **'source and summit'** of the People of God.

If you don't normally thank God for your food at meal times you might like to introduce this, and add a prayer for those who haven't enough to eat.

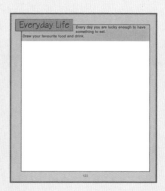

Page 125 Old Testament

There won't be enough time to remind the children of the whole story of humanity as seen through the eyes of the Jewish people. You could go back over the whole book (or better still, a children's Bible) and trace the story from Adam and Eve to the entry into the Promised Land. When the people were in the Promised Land they had time to work out their laws, traditions, feasts, etc. In fact it was only after they settled down that they wrote down the stories of Adam and Eve, Abraham etc.

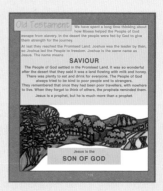

Page 126 New Testament

This story, like the one of Emmaus last session, is a **'model'** of the Eucharist. Christ feeds us (note that the apostles, including trained fishermen, couldn't catch fish themselves) and asks us to do likewise (*Feed my lambs and sheep*). There are many other stories you could tell your children about how we bring about the Kingdom of God (how we enter the Promised Land). For example: *"I was hungry and you gave me food"* is a good one. *Matthew. 25:34-40*

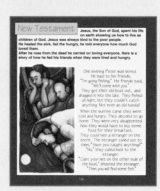

Page 128 Picture to colour in

Page 129 Church

Sometimes people say they don't go to church as they are just as good as church-goers, or even that church-goers are hypocrites. This may be true, as we are a Church of sinners, but the Eucharist, properly understood, strengthens us to serve others. What we put into it, and what we receive from it has a direct bearing on how we live every day.

Your child has prepared for the Eucharist, and received Holy Communion. The leaders hope that the children, and you, have all enjoyed the Course. There is so much to learn, and we will never understand the glory of the Eucharist in this life. However, we cannot know God by the intellect. It is the heart that understands and loves.

May God bless you and your family.

Dear Grandparent,

You are reading this because your grandchild is preparing for his/her First Holy Communion. You may be a silver-haired old grandad a glamourous young granny, or somebody quite different. You may be a devout church-goer, an atheist, or something in between these two. But whoever or whatever you are, your grandchild is taking an important step in preparing for First Holy Communion, and your loving involvement can enrich the whole process.

Your grandchild's first steps

A child's first steps are very precious. You can probably remember when your own child was learning to walk, and if you were lucky you were there when your grandchild began to toddle. You had to decide how much help to give, and when to let go. There were many tumbles, but with some tears, and much laughter the infant began to walk. You may have had mixed feelings as your child grew from dependency to independence.

You may also have mixed feelings as your grandchild takes the step of preparing for First Holy Communion It will depend on your relationship with the Church. You may be delighted, dubious or aghast at the idea! If your feelings are different to that of the child's parent(s) this could be a complication, and you will need to use the wisdom and diplomacy that come with maturity.

Freedom of choice

If your journey towards wholeness and fulfilment follows a different path than your grandchild, please remember that - with his parent(s) - he/she has decided to walk in full communion with the Church, and to be nourished in that journey by Jesus, the bread of life. No matter how painful this may be, please respect his/her freedom to choose, and take an interest in your grandchild's preparation. If you feel badly towards the Church, you may find that a closer look gives you a pleasant surprise.

Perhaps you are a fully committed church member, and have had to do a lot of running around to ensure that your grandchild is brought up as a Christian because your own child does not go to church often. If you are reading this letter, you have probably succeeded in getting your grandchild enrolled in preparation sessions, but tact will be necessary here also. Just as you can't force a baby to walk before he is ready, so you can't force a child to love God in the way you do. You need the wisdom to know when to encourage and when to stand back. Pray for your grandchild and his/her family. Keep up to date with Church teaching so that you can answer questions if necessary.

New insights

If you are a regular church-goer and so is your family, you are in a happy position. Not only can your faith be a shining example to everyone, you will probably find that your grandchild will give you new insights into the Eucharist. Children have an uncanny knack of asking very searching questions. You may find that as you search for answers your relationship with Christ takes on a new lease of life you didn't think was possible.

The following thoughts may help you understand more fully the important step your grandchild is taking, and how closely you are involved.

- Love cannot contain itself and one of the fruits of your love for your partner was your child. Just as Jesus said to those he loved at the Last Supper, you said to your partner, "**This is my body, given for you**". This giving was not a one-off thing, but a way of life. Now you can look back and see how, in the good times and the bad times, your body has been given, your life's blood has been poured out for those you love. Your giving of your life was, literally, life-giving.

- Your body may not be all that it once was! Like Jesus, you bear the marks of love, of daily sacrifice for your family. But like Jesus, you live to see the fruits of that love - the love that will not contain itself, but is reborn in your children and your children's children.

In the next few months your grandchild is going to reflect more and more on the life-giving love God gives us in Jesus, and which is shown most clearly in the Eucharist, the Sacrament of Love. Your grandchild will discover how he or she is part of the divine plan of love, and that by sharing in the Eucharist he is strengthened to love God, his/her family, and the whole world. You and your grandchild are caught up in this mystery. Enjoy this time of preparation together, and enjoy the life-giving fruits of the Eucharist.

Notes for the First Holy Communion Day

Notes for the First Holy Communion Day